FOUNDATIONS

MISSIONAL COMMUNITY GUIDEBOOK

D1319569

MULTIPLICATION
PRESS

Foundations: Missional Community Guidebook

Copyright © 2013 Robert C. McNabb

Second Printing

ISBN 978-1-942374-02-2

CONTENTS

PURPOSE

WHO SHOULD USE THIS GUIDEBOOK?

- Disciples who are ready to enter into the adventure of team evangelism
- People who are able to fulfill the requirements of the Team Covenant (next page)
- Believers who desire a deeper and more consistent walk with the Lord

WHAT ARE SOME OF THE MAJOR LEARNING OBJECTIVES OF THIS STUDY?

Participants will gain the following:

- Firm establishment in their faith
- The ability to witness for Christ more effectively
- More meaningful and consistent times alone with God
- Basic Bible interpretation skills
- A greater understanding of their mission in life
- A more victorious Christian life
- Increased impact on the lost

HOW IS THIS GUIDEBOOK DIFFERENT FROM OTHER DISCIPLESHIP MATERIALS?

Most discipleship materials focus on knowledge acquisition. Their primary focus is to learn. The hope is that after learning, you will start doing. This guidebook is different. The focus is on doing and building habits. As you build these habits, you will learn, and you will keep learning long after you finish these materials. The habits that you will work together to establish are:

- Daily time with God (self-feeding on his Word)
- Evangelism
- Prayer for the Lost
- Scripture Memory
- Obedience
- Teamwork

INTRODUCTION

A MISSIONAL COMMUNITY IS A DISCIPLE-MAKING TEAM

The term "Missional Community" has become very popular. Because of this, it is used to mean a wide variety of things. With this in mind, we have chosen to use the term "disciple-making team" frequently in these materials as a clarifying synonym for missional community.

HOW IS A DISCIPLE-MAKING TEAM DIFFERENT FROM A SMALL-GROUP?

The purpose of a disciple-making team is to glorify God by making disciples of all nations. Increasing our biblical knowledge is not the goal, but that will happen. The purpose is not to fellowship and pray, although we will do those things. Finally, the purpose is not to hold us accountable to spiritual disciplines, though that will occur when we meet. As you can see, a disciple-making team differs from a small group, a discipleship group, a Bible study, or a prayer group. Of course, there is nothing wrong with being part of any of those types of groups.

Disciple-making teams are different in that they seek to stay focused on fulfilling the Great Commission through the multiplication of disciple-makers. This focus drives members into deeper times of fellowship, prayer, Bible study, and accountability as the team lives and ministers together in a missional community. Mission is not one of the purposes of the team; it is the reason the team exists.

TEAM COVENANT

By God's grace, I covenant with the other members of my team to:

- Spend at least three hours with Jesus each week.

- Spend at least two hours reaching out to the lost each week.

- Spend at least one hour in prayer for my lost friends and the world with others of this team each week.

- Arrive prepared and ready to contribute to the group each weekly Half-Time meeting.

- Begin discipling others within a few months of completing this study.

I will strive, by the grace of God, to meet the above commitments.

Signed _____ Date _____/ _____/ _____

HOW CAN THIS GROUP DEVELOP LEADERS?

First, find an apprentice or co-leader who will help you lead the group. Hopefully, doing this with you will help prepare them to lead their own group soon.

Ideally, there will be at least two or three people out of the six to twelve in the group whom you can challenge to join as your apprentices.

The best people to consider for this are ones who:

- Have been established in their faith
- Have displayed faithfulness in passing on what they are taught
- Are teachable to you
- Have the availability to help you lead the group

Your strategy should be to spend extra time with these apprentices (like Jesus did with Peter, James, and John) and equip them to help lead the others in the community. This gets you discipling people in the context of ministry.

HOW TO CHALLENGE SOMEONE INTO THIS GROUP

PRAY AND ASK GOD TO BRING TO MIND THE NAMES OF SIX TO TWELVE PEOPLE WHO:

Are already established in their faith.

Seem eager to evangelize and make disciples.

SCHEDULE AN APPOINTMENT WITH THOSE YOU WILL CHALLENGE ONTO THE TEAM:

Use the Sharing the Vision tool (p.102).

Go over the Purpose page and Team Covenant.

Take along one of your apprentices if possible.

SET A DATE BY WHICH THEY MUST DECIDE.

WEEKLY 3-2-1

3 HOURS *with Jesus*

Everything begins with God. The foundation of a healthy personal ministry must be our own relationship with Christ. Therefore, commit to communing with him through prayer, worship, and reading his Word at least three hours a week.

2 HOURS *with the lost*

In order to reap, we must sow the seed of the gospel. We will spend at least two hours a week finding lost people, generating interest in Jesus, sharing the gospel, and Lord willing, helping them decide to follow Christ. Jesus sent his disciples two-by-two. In the same way, we want to go out two-by-two with other people on our team. We may not share the gospel every time, but we will always do something evangelistic, like meeting new people, sharing our testimonies, praying for people's needs, or inviting them to experience our community.

1 HOUR *corporate prayer*

Jesus informs us that the key to the harvest is prayer. To see people enter into the Kingdom of God, we must become a people dedicated to prayer both privately and corporately. As a community, we will dedicate at least one hour of corporate prayer for the lost and the nations each week.

HALF-TIME

When it comes to spiritual multiplication, what happens all week long is more important than what happens in a once-a-week meeting. That's why we call our meetings "Half-Time." They're simply an opportunity to pause once a week and report on what God has been doing in the last six days. During Half-Time, we will pray and encourage one another, plan our next week of ministry, and discuss the week's reading assignments.

WELCOME || *15 minutes*

The Welcome portion will provide an opportunity to learn about the other people in our community. Each week, we will have a different icebreaker question to discuss.

WITNESS || *10 minutes*

The Witness time is an opportunity to share testimonies about what God did the previous week in our personal lives or in the lives of our family and friends (testimonies of what happened with our lost friends will occur during the Works section). Be sure to write down a few notes in your workbook so you can look back and remember what God has done.

WORSHIP || *10 minutes*

The Worship time is for our group to pray, sing, talk, or praise God in any other way that seems fitting to worship Him for who he is and what he has done.

WORKS || *25 minutes*

The Works time is for our group to share about what God is doing among our lost friends and plan for the next week's ministry.

Each week, we will write names of our lost friends on a large piece of light blue poster board or fabric called "Big Blue." (You can read "The Legend of Big Blue" on p. 99.) Names should only be added once we have a person's phone number and are likely to see them again. We will underline names of friends we are reading the Bible with, and put a cross next to any people who start following Christ.

You will also start adding some of these names to your FISHing chart (p. 95) as you begin to share with them.

We will share how our ministry went in the past week and talk about any plans we need to make for the upcoming week.

We will then spend time in prayer for our lost friends and our plans for the week.

INTRODUCTION

WORLD || *10 minutes*

The World time will help us learn a little more about how God views the world in which we live. Each week, we will spend some time learning more about and praying for the world around us during **Pray for the Nations.**

WORD || *20 minutes*

The Word time gives our community an opportunity to discuss the Daily Quiet Times and Learning Questions. This time will also be used to review our Key Verse. Then we will learn more about personal Bible study by reading **Sharpening Your Skills.**

GAME PLAN

This is a convenient list of everything we need to do before next week's Half-Time.

DAILY QUIET TIMES

Each week, we will have a set of Daily Quiet Times to guide our three hours of time with God. Each of us should read the verses in context to get the full picture of what is being said.

LEARNING QUESTIONS

Each week, you will have a set of questions that go along with your Daily Quiet Times. We will discuss these during Half-Time each week.

KEY VERSE

These are important verses that come from our weekly readings. Each week, we will memorize the assigned verse and be prepared to recite it at the Half-Time meeting.

MY STORY

HALF-TIME || WEEK 1

WELCOME || 15 MINUTES

Have everyone briefly introduce themselves (one minute) and answer:

> Why do you want to be in a disciple-making team?

Take some time to familiarize yourselves with this entire workbook.

Together, read through and discuss the *Introduction* (p. 1-6).

Sign the *Covenant* (p. 2).

WORKS || 25 MINUTES

FISHING CHART

Turn to the FISHing chart (p. 95). Take a few minutes to write down the names of your lost friends and relatives who live in the same town as you. If you see you don't have ten, then make a plan to meet new people this week.

BIG BLUE

As a group, write the names of your lost friends on the large piece of poster board or fabric we call "Big Blue." After all the names are written, circle around and pray for your friends.

TOOLS

The leader should introduce "My Story" (p. 97) and then demonstrate how to share it. You will be working on your story throughout this week and will practice sharing it at Half-Time next week.

ACTIVITY

Spend some time praying for your team, for the lost friends you already have and for the new friends you will meet.

Turn to the Game Plan on the next page and fill in your goals for this week.

GAME PLAN FOR NEXT WEEK

3 HOURS *with Jesus*

Daily Quiet Times and Discussion Questions
Memorize Romans 6:23

2 HOURS *with lost people*

I will meet _____ new people this week

1 HOUR *corporate prayer*

This week I will pray with _____

LEARNING ASSIGNMENT

Complete "My Story: Interest-Creating Testimony" worksheet (p. 97)

THE GOSPEL

There is nothing more important than understanding the gospel. Properly responding to the gospel leads us to salvation. It is also the means by which we walk with Christ and grow in our love relationship with him. It is critical for us to understand the gospel clearly so that we can share it with others. There is probably more to the gospel than you have realized before. Ask God to open your eyes this week and be prepared to discover that the gospel is even better than you think!

KEY VERSE: Romans 6:23

DAY 1: John 3:13-18, Mark 1:14-15, Acts 20:21

What is the gospel (good news) that you find in these verses?

What do these verses mention as separating men from God?

What is the appropriate response to the gospel?

PRAYER

Today I thank God for...

Today I am asking God for...

Learn this week's Key Verse.

DAY 2: 1 Corinthians 15:3-7

What are the important points of the gospel mentioned in verses 3-4?

Why do you think Paul felt it was important to mention that there were witnesses to the resurrection?

How will you respond today to the truths presented in these verses?

PRAYER

Today I thank God for...

Today I am asking God for...

Review the Key Verse.

DAY 3: 1 Corinthians 2:1-2, Matthew 13:44

In 1 Corinthians 2:2, we see that Paul did not just preach the good news about how we can be saved ("him crucified"). He also preached "Jesus Christ" as the gospel. List below some ways that the person of Christ is good news.

From Matthew 13:44, how valuable should we consider the kingdom of God? Why?

What should our response be to the gospel of the kingdom?

PRAYER

Today I thank God for...

Today I am asking God for...

Review the Key Verse.

DAY 4: Ephesians 2:1-9

What is the condition of man without Christ?

How is God described in these verses?

What must we do to be saved?

PRAYER

Today I thank God for...

Today I am asking God for...

Review the Key Verse.

DAY 5: Romans 6:23, Titus 3:5

What do these verses teach about how one can be saved?

Whom will you share this good news with today?

PRAYER

Today I thank God for...

Today I am asking God for...

Review the Key Verse.

DAY 6: 2 Corinthians 5:14-21

List the points of good news you find in these verses.

According to these verses, what must we do if we really believe the gospel?

Whom will you share the gospel with today?

PRAYER

Today I thank God for...

Today I am asking God for...

Review the Key Verse.

DAY 7: Summary and Reflection Day

After looking back over your quiet times for the week, summarize what God has been teaching you.

What specific action will you take to apply what you have learned?

PRAYER

Today I thank God for...

Today I am asking God for...

Write out this week's Key Verse below:

THE GOSPEL

Answer these questions as well as you can before the Half-Time meeting. You will discuss them as a team during the Word time.

1. How would you answer someone who asks, "What must I believe and do to be saved?"

2. What is the required response to the gospel?

3. Why did Jesus preach about the "kingdom of God" when he shared the good news?

4. How is Jesus the gospel? (Mark 1:1)

5. How confident are you that you have truly repented (surrendered) and believed (trusted)?

WELCOME || 15 MINUTES

Have each person answer the question:

Who has had the greatest impact on your spiritual life?

Split into pairs and share your story with a partner, giving each other feedback on how to make your story more clear or interest-creating.

WITNESS || 10 MINUTES

What did you see God do this week?

WORSHIP || 10 MINUTES

Thank God together in prayer for what he did last week.

Use an iPod, guitar, etc. and sing a few songs together.

WORKS || 25 MINUTES

FISHING CHART

Turn to the FISHing chart (p. 95) and write names of your lost friends on it.

The ideal people to have on your FISHing Chart are people:

Whom you will be able to see repeatedly

Who would be open to your influence

Discuss as a team where and how each of you can meet people who fulfill the two criteria above.

It's okay if you can't fill the chart this week. You will be working as a team to fill in new people in the coming weeks.

Turn to p. 98 and read about asking questions. Then decide how many people you will share your story with this week. Write it in the Game Plan.

BIG BLUE

Get out your Big Blue and write the names of your team's lost friends. When all the names have been written, put it in the middle of the group and pray for those listed. Do not hurry this prayer time. It is the life blood of your ministry as a team and should therefore be central in each of your meetings.

ACTIVITY

Turn to the Game Plan on the next page and fill in your goals for this week.

WORLD || 10 MINUTES

PRAY FOR THE NATIONS

Pray for the 2.90 billion people who currently live beyond the reach of the gospel.[1]

WORD || 20 MINUTES

Share Romans 6:23 with a partner.

Discuss your Daily Quiet Times using the Learning Questions.

Read and discuss the "Sharpening Your Skills" tip below.

SHARPENING YOUR SKILLS:
Principle of Context

Each verse or passage should be interpreted in light of the context of the chapter and book in which it is found. Some Christians say that denying oneself, taking up one's cross daily, and following Jesus (Luke 9:23) is an optional act of discipleship and thus not required for salvation. Read Luke 9:23 along with Luke 9:24-25 and discuss if these verses (the context) help clear up whether or not this type of total surrender to Christ is necessary for salvation.

GAME PLAN FOR NEXT WEEK

3 HOURS *with Jesus*

Daily Quiet Times and Discussion Questions
Memorize 1 John 5:11-13

2 HOURS *with lost people*

I will meet _____ new people this week

I will share my story with _____ people this week

My ministry partner this week will be _____

1 HOUR *corporate prayer*

This week I will pray with _____

ASSURANCE OF SALVATION

Going through life without assurance of your eternal salvation can cause many mental, emotional, and spiritual problems. More dangerous than that, though, is going through life with a false sense of assurance. Thankfully, the Bible speaks clearly on this subject. By studying what it teaches and engaging in honest evaluation, we may gain great confidence in our salvation or insight into our need for it.

KEY VERSE: 1 John 5:11-13

DAY 1: Matthew 7:21-23, Titus 1:16, 1 Corinthians 6:9-11

Is it possible to be deceived into having a false assurance of salvation?

What relationship do you see between works and salvation in these verses?

PRAYER

Today I thank God for...

Today I am asking God for...

Learn this week's Key Verse.

DAY 2: 1 John 5:13, 3:18-20

Is it possible to have a proper assurance of salvation?

Why does John say he wrote the book of 1 John?

What is your application step for today?

PRAYER

Today I thank God for...

Today I am asking God for...

Review the Key Verse.

DAY 3: What tests of true salvation does John offer?

1 John 1:6-7

1 John 2:3-6

1 John 1:8-10

1 John 2:9-10

How will you obey Jesus today?

PRAYER

Today I thank God for...

Today I am asking God for...

Review the Key Verse.

DAY 4: What tests of true salvation does John offer?

1 John 2:15

1 John 3:3, 6, 9

1 John 2:23

1 John 3:23-24

How will you obey Jesus today?

PRAYER

Today I thank God for...

Today I am asking God for...

Review the Key Verse.

DAY 5: Galatians 5:19-23

List out the acts of the flesh (sinful nature) and the fruit of the spirit.

Flesh		Spirit	
_____	_____	_____	_____
_____	_____	_____	_____
_____	_____	_____	_____
_____	_____	_____	_____
_____	_____	_____	
_____	_____		
_____	_____		
_____	_____		

Do you see God's spirit working in your life—moving you away from the flesh and increasingly toward a life full of the fruit of the Spirit?

PRAYER

Today I thank God for...

Today I am asking God for...

Review the Key Verse.

DAY 6: Philippians 1:6, 2:13; 2 Timothy 1:12; 1 John 2:19

How does the grace of God work in you after you are saved?

Once someone is truly saved, can they ever completely walk away from God?

What truths from these verses will you seek to dwell on today?

PRAYER

Today I thank God for...

Today I am asking God for...

Review the Key Verse.

DAY 7: Summary and Reflection Day

After looking back over your quiet times for the week, summarize what God has been teaching you.

Read 2 Corinthians 13:5. What are you told to do?

Review this week's verses and examine yourself. How confident are you that you are "in the faith"? _____%

PRAYER

Today I thank God for...

Today I am asking God for...

Write out this week's Key Verse below:

ASSURANCE OF SALVATION

Answer these questions as well as you can before the Half-Time meeting. You will discuss them as a team during the Word time.

1. Is it possible to have a false assurance of salvation? Explain.

2. Is it possible to have an accurate assurance of salvation? Explain.

3. What do the Scriptures teach about how we can know if we are saved or not?

4. Will Christians continue to sin after they are saved?

5. Should people have assurance of salvation if they don't fight against sin in their lives?

HALF-TIME || WEEK 3

WELCOME || 15 MINUTES

Have each person answer the question:

What is one book (besides the Bible) that has impacted your spiritual life?

Split into pairs and share your story with a new partner, giving each other feedback on how to make your story more clear or interest-creating.

WITNESS || 10 MINUTES

What did you see God do this week?

WORSHIP || 10 MINUTES

Thank God together in prayer for what he did last week.

Make a list of the names of God and praise him for his attributes.

WORKS || 25 MINUTES

FISHING CHART

Update your FISHing chart with any new people you met this week or steps you took in the FISHing process.

BIG BLUE

Add your team's new friends to Big Blue. Put the list in the middle of the group and pray over your friends.

ACTIVITY

Turn to p. 99 and read about a Matthew Party. Spend some time as a group planning one together.

Turn to the Game Plan on the next page and fill in your goals for this week.

WORLD || 10 MINUTES

PRAY FOR THE NATIONS

Pray for the 209 million people who do not have a single word of Scripture in their language.[6]

WORD || 20 MINUTES

Share 1 John 5:11-13 with a partner.

Discuss your Daily Quiet Times using the Learning Questions.

Read and discuss the "Sharpening Your Skills" tip below.

SHARPENING YOUR SKILLS:
Spiritual Discernment

Spiritual discernment is required to understand the truths of God. Read 1 Corinthians 2:12-14 together and then discuss the importance of prayerful dependence on the Spirit as a prerequisite for correct Bible interpretation and application.

GAME PLAN FOR NEXT WEEK

3 HOURS *with Jesus*

Daily Quiet Times and Discussion Questions
Memorize Luke 9:23-25

2 HOURS *with lost people*

I will meet _____ new people this week

I will share my story with _____ people this week

My ministry partner this week will be _____

Plan a Matthew Party

1 HOUR *corporate prayer*

This week I will pray with _____

WEEK 4

FOLLOWING CHRIST AS LORD

Subjecting yourself to someone else and obeying their will and commands doesn't sound that attractive, does it? But what if the person giving the orders is all-wise and all-loving? What if their commands actually benefit you and their will is for your good? Ask God this week to lead you into a joyful submission to his Lordship.

KEY VERSE: Luke 9:23-25

DAY 1: Luke 9:23-25

What does Jesus say is required of anyone who wants to "save his life"?

What do we gain by surrendering the control of our lives to Christ?

What logical reason does Jesus give for dying to yourself and following him?

Are there any areas of your life that are not surrendered to the Lordship of Christ? Are you willing to surrender them now? Why or why not?

PRAYER

Today I thank God for...

Today I am asking God for...

Learn this week's Key Verse.

DAY 2: James 1:22-25

What are the dangers of disobedience?

What are the benefits of obedience?

Is there an area of your life in which you are living in disobedience to God?

What step of obedience will you take today?

PRAYER

Today I thank God for...

Today I am asking God for...

Review the Key Verse.

DAY 3: Matthew 7:24-27

What is the result of obedience mentioned in these verses?

What will be the result of disobedience?

Ask God to show you some way that you need to obey him today and write it below.

PRAYER

Today I thank God for...

Today I am asking God for...

Review the Key Verse.

DAY 4: 1 John 5:2-3

What is the relationship between loving God and obeying God?

Why do you think John says "his commandments are not burdensome"?

Have you been viewing obedience to God as a chore or an act of love and a benefit to you?

PRAYER

Today I thank God for...

Today I am asking God for...

Review the Key Verse.

DAY 5: Luke 14:25-33

What did Jesus say we must do if we want to become his disciple?

v. 26

v. 27

v. 33

Why does Jesus recommend counting the cost before beginning to follow him?

Have you completely surrendered every area of your life to Christ?

How will you apply this passage to your life today?

PRAYER

Today I thank God for...

Today I am asking God for...

Review the Key Verse.

DAY 6: Hebrews 10:19-23, 1 John 1:8-2:2

What should we do when we realize we have disobeyed?

What reasons do these verses mention for you to have confidence in approaching God even after you have disobeyed?

Be still and ask God to show you any sin in your life. Then confess it and pray for his strength to turn away from it.

PRAYER

Today I thank God for...

Today I am asking God for...

Review the Key Verse.

DAY 7: Summary and Reflection Day

After looking back over your quiet times for the week, summarize what God has been teaching you.

What specific action will you take to apply what you have learned?

PRAYER

Today I thank God for...

Today I am asking God for...

Write out this week's Key Verse below:

LORDSHIP AND OBEDIENCE

Answer these questions as well as you can before the Half-Time meeting. You will discuss them as a team during the Word time.

1. What does it mean to make Jesus the Lord of your life?

2. Is surrender to the Lordship of Christ required for salvation? (Luke 9:23-25, 14:25-35)

3. Would you say that you have completely surrendered your life to Christ?

4. How have you viewed obedience to God recently—as a burden or a joy?

5. What steps of obedience do you feel you need to take as a result of your time in the Word this week?

HALF-TIME || WEEK 4

WELCOME || 15 MINUTES

Have each person answer the question:

What songs are included on the soundtrack to your life?

Split into pairs and share your story with a new partner, giving each other feedback on how to make your story more clear or interest-creating.

WITNESS || 10 MINUTES

What did you see God do this week?

WORSHIP || 10 MINUTES

Thank God together in prayer for what he did last week.

Read Psalm 136 responsively: one person reads the first half of a verse, and everyone reads the second half together.

WORKS || 25 MINUTES

FISHING CHART

Update your FISHing chart with any new people you met this week or steps you took in the FISHing process.

BIG BLUE

Add your team's new friends to Big Blue. Put the list in the middle of the group and pray over your friends.

ACTIVITY

Turn to the Game Plan on the next page and fill in your goals for this week.

WORLD || 10 MINUTES

PRAY FOR THE NATIONS

Pray for the 2.82 billion unreached people who live in the 10/40 Window (the rectangular area of North Africa, the Middle East, and Asia approximately between 10 degrees north and 40 degrees north latitude.)[1]

WORD || 20 MINUTES

Share Luke 9:23-25 with a partner.

Discuss your Daily Quiet Times using the Learning Questions.

Read and discuss the "Sharpening Your Skills" tip below.

SHARPENING YOUR SKILLS:
Principle of Application

God gave his Word not just to increase our knowledge, but to change our lives. God-pleasing and life-changing Bible study must include an intent to apply whatever is learned in joyful obedience to Christ. Read James 1:22-25 and 1 Corinthians 8:1. Discuss the dangers of Bible study devoid of application.

GAME PLAN FOR NEXT WEEK

3 HOURS *with Jesus*

Daily Quiet Times and Discussion Questions
Memorize 2 Corinthians 5:17

2 HOURS *with lost people*

I will meet _____ new people this week

I will share my story with _____ people this week

My ministry partner this week will be _____

1 HOUR *corporate prayer*

This week I will pray with _____

WEEK 5

IDENTITY IN CHRIST

Your past shame is not your present identity. When you were born again, you became a new person in Christ. You were adopted as God's child and now have all the rights and privileges of a son or daughter. You were legally cleared of all guilt. You are no longer subject to condemnation for your sins—past, present, or future. Though you will still have struggles with sin, he has set you free from its power, and you can now experience freedom in your life that you never dreamed possible.

It is important for us to understand the truth about who we are in Christ so that we can be free to live up to our true position before him. Prepare to be encouraged by the truth of who you are in Christ!

KEY VERSE: 2 Corinthians 5:17

DAY 1:

John 1:12   I am a _____ again.

John 3:3   I am _____.

John 8:36   I am _____.

John 15:15   I am a _____ of Jesus

How will you respond?

PRAYER

Today I thank God for...

Today I am asking God for...

Learn this week's Key Verse.

DAY 2:

Ephesians 1:3   I am _____ with every spiritual blessing.

Ephesians 1:4   I am _____ by God.

Ephesians 1:4   I am _____ and _____ before God.

Ephesians 1:5   I am _____ to be his _____.

Ephesians 1:7   I am _____ by his blood.

How will you respond?

PRAYER

Today I thank God for...

Today I am asking God for...

Review the Key Verse.

DAY 3:

    Colossians 1:13   I am a citizen of _____.

    Colossians 1:14   I am _____ of my sins.

    Colossians 1:22   I am _____ to God.

    Colossians 1:22   I am _____ before God.

How will you respond?

PRAYER

Today I thank God for...

Today I am asking God for...

Review the Key Verse.

DAY 4:

    Colossians 2:10   I am _____ (complete) in Christ.

    Colossians 2:13   I am _____ together with Christ.

    Colossians 3:1   I am _____ with Christ.

    Colossians 3:12   I am _____ by God.

How will you respond?

PRAYER

Today I thank God for...

Today I am asking God for...

Review the Key Verse.

DAY 5:

Romans 5:1   I have been _____.

Romans 8:1-2   I am _____ from condemnation.

Romans 8:28   I am assured that God works for my _____ in all circumstances.

Romans 8:38-39   I cannot be separated from the _____ of God.

How will you respond?

PRAYER

Today I thank God for...

Today I am asking God for...

Review the Key Verse.

DAY 6:

1 Corinthians 3:16   I am God's _____.

2 Corinthians 5:17   I am a _____.

2 Corinthians 5:20   I am Christ's _____.

1 Corinthians 12:27 I am a member of Christ's _____.

How will you respond?

PRAYER

Today I thank God for...

Today I am asking God for...

Review the Key Verse.

DAY 7: Summary and Reflection Day

After looking back over your quiet times for the week, summarize what God has been teaching you.

What specific action will you take to apply what you have learned?

PRAYER

Today I thank God for...

Today I am asking God for...

Write out this week's Key Verse below:

IDENTITY IN CHRIST

Answer these questions as well as you can before the Half-Time meeting. You will discuss them as a team during the Word time.

1. Why is it important to understand who you are in Christ?

2. Which identity statements resonated most with you? Why?

3. What response will you have to the truth of who Christ has made you to be?

4. Who would benefit from you sharing with them what you learned this week?

HALF-TIME || WEEK 5

WELCOME || 15 MINUTES

Have each person answer the question:

What have you found to be most helpful in spending quality time alone fellowshipping with God?

Split into pairs and share your story with a new partner, giving each other feedback on how to make your story more clear or interest-creating.

WITNESS || 10 MINUTES

What did you see God do this week?

WORSHIP || 10 MINUTES

Thank God together in prayer for what he did last week.

Have a time of silence before the Lord to hear His voice and worship. Then share with one another what you heard.

WORKS || 25 MINUTES

FISHING CHART
Update your FISHing chart with any new people you met this week or steps you took in the FISHing process.

BIG BLUE
Add your team's new friends to Big Blue. Put the list in the middle of the group and pray over your friends.

ACTIVITY
Turn to the Game Plan on the next page and fill in your goals for this week.

WORLD || 10 MINUTES

PRAY FOR THE NATIONS

Pray for the 161 million people who live in Tribal people groups.[2]

WORD || 20 MINUTES

Share 2 Corinthians 5:17 with a partner.

Discuss your Daily Quiet Times using the Learning Questions.

Read and discuss the "Sharpening Your Skills" tip below.

SHARPENING YOUR SKILLS:
Principle of Inspiration

Always approach the Bible with the remembrance that it is God's inspired and infallible Word. Submit yourself to God as you read his Word and ask him to use it to teach you, correct you, train you, and equip you for ministry. Read 2 Timothy 3:16-17 and discuss the proper attitude with which we should approach God's Word.

GAME PLAN FOR NEXT WEEK

3 HOURS *with Jesus*

Daily Quiet Times and Discussion Questions
Memorize Matthew 28:19-20

2 HOURS *with lost people*

I will meet _____ new people this week

I will share my story with _____ people this week

My ministry partner this week will be _____

1 HOUR *corporate prayer*

This week I will pray with _____

PURPOSE IN LIFE

We were created to glorify God. The more we get to know and find our satisfaction in him, the more the world sees how worthy he is. As we share the gospel with people and make disciples of all nations, God's glory and fame spread throughout the earth. Before sin entered the world, man was commanded to "be fruitful and multiply," thus filling the world with God's image bearers (his glory). Today our purpose is the same: to glorify God by spreading a passion for him to all peoples.

What about you? Will you fulfill your God-given purpose in life or chase the temporal things this world has to offer?

KEY VERSE: Matthew 28:19-20

DAY 1: Isaiah 43:6-7, 1 Corinthians 10:31, Genesis 1:28

Why did God create us?

How is the command to "be fruitful and multiply and fill the earth" related to our glorifying God?

What will you do today to glorify God?

PRAYER

Today I thank God for...

Today I am asking God for...

Learn this week's Key Verse.

DAY 2: Genesis 12:1-3, Galatians 3:7-9

Why was Abraham blessed? (Genesis 12:1-3)

Should you consider yourself blessed? Why or why not? (Galatians 3:7-9)

In what ways, if any, are you pursuing hard after eternally significant things?

What changes do you need to make in how you spend your time and money?

PRAYER

Today I thank God for...

Today I am asking God for...

Review the Key Verse.

DAY 3: Acts 20:24, Romans 15:20-21

What did Paul see as his mission in life?

How do these verses reveal God's heart for the nations?

What do you think you could do with your life to spread God's story to people groups who have never heard of Jesus?

PRAYER

Today I thank God for...

Today I am asking God for...

Review the Key Verse.

DAY 4: Matthew 6:19-21, 1 Thessalonians 2:19-20

What are true, eternal treasures?

In what ways, if any, are you pursuing hard after eternally significant things?

What changes do you need to make in how you spend your time and money?

PRAYER

Today I thank God for...

Today I am asking God for...

Review the Key Verse.

DAY 5: Matthew 24:14, 28:18-20; Acts 1:8

How do you see God's heart for the nations in these verses?

What do you need to do in order to align your life with God's heart?

PRAYER

Today I thank God for...

Today I am asking God for...

Review the Key Verse.

DAY 6: Revelation 5:9, 7:9

How do you see God's heart for the nations in these verses?

What do you need to do in order to align your life with God's heart?

PRAYER

Today I thank God for...

Today I am asking God for...

Review the Key Verse.

DAY 7: Summary and Reflection Day

After looking back over your quiet times for the week, summarize what God has been teaching you.

What specific action will you take to apply what you have learned?

PRAYER

Today I thank God for...

Today I am asking God for...

Write out this week's Key Verse below:

PURPOSE IN LIFE

Answer these questions as well as you can before the Half-Time meeting. You will discuss them as a team during the Word time.

1. What did you learn this week about God's heart for the nations?

2. Why should getting the gospel to those who have never heard be a top priority in our lives?

3. Describe your purpose in life in a sentence.

4. What do you need to do in order to align your life with God's heart?

HALF-TIME || WEEK 6

WELCOME || 15 MINUTES

Share about something you did that made you feel you were doing what God created you to do.

WITNESS || 10 MINUTES

What did you see God do this week?

WORSHIP || 10 MINUTES

Thank God together in prayer for what he did last week.

Use an iPod, guitar, etc. and sing a few songs together.

WORKS || 25 MINUTES

FISHING CHART
Update your FISHing chart with any new people you met this week or steps you took in the FISHing process.

BIG BLUE
Add your team's new friends to Big Blue. Put the list in the middle of the group and pray over your friends.

TOOLS
The leader should introduce "The Bridge Illustration" (p. 100) and then demonstrate how to share it.

Pair up and practice The Bridge with another teammate, giving each other feedback.

ACTIVITY
Plan another Matthew Party as a group.

Turn to the Game Plan on the next page and fill in your goals for this week.

WORLD || 10 MINUTES

PRAY FOR THE NATIONS
Pray for the 860 million people who live in Hindu people groups.[2]

WORD || 20 MINUTES

Share Matthew 28:18-20 with a partner.

Discuss your Daily Quiet Times using the Learning Questions.

Read and discuss the "Sharpening Your Skills" tip below.

> **SHARPENING YOUR SKILLS:**
> Principle of Original Intent
>
> For us to properly understand and apply the Bible to our daily lives, we must understand what the author intended to communicate to the original readers of his message. Discuss together why it is important to understand the historical and cultural context of the original readers of the Bible.

GAME PLAN FOR NEXT WEEK

3 HOURS *with Jesus*

Daily Quiet Times and Discussion Questions
Memorize Mark 1:35

2 HOURS *with lost people*

I will meet _____ new people this week

I will share The Bridge with _____ people this week

My ministry partner this week will be _____

Plan a Matthew Party

1 HOUR *corporate prayer*

This week I will pray with _____

WEEK 7

QUIET TIME

There is no greater privilege in the world than having a personal relationship with the creator of the universe and the king of kings. To neglect such an opportunity would be crazy. Pray that God would show you this week how to truly meet with him in your quiet times and how to interact with him in worshipful and life-changing ways.

KEY VERSE: Mark 1:35

DAY 1: Mark 1:35

Answer all relevant observation questions. (Some passages may not have answers for all.)

OBSERVATION

Who?   Where?

What?   When?

How?   Why?

INTERPRETATION: What does God intend for me to learn from this passage?

APPLICATION: I will obey what is taught here by...

MULTIPLICATION: I will share what I've learned with _____.

PRAYER

Today I thank God for...

Today I am asking God for...

Learn this week's Key Verse.

DAY 2: Psalm 84:1-10

OBSERVATION

Who?   Where?

What?   When?

How?   Why?

INTERPRETATION: What does God intend for me to learn from this passage?

APPLICATION: I will obey what is taught here by...

MULTIPLICATION: I will share what I've learned with _____.

PRAYER

Today I thank God for...

Today I am asking God for...

Review the Key Verse.

DAY 3: Luke 10:38-42

OBSERVATION

Who?   Where?

What?   When?

How?   Why?

INTERPRETATION: What does God intend for me to learn from this passage?

APPLICATION: I will obey what is taught here by...

MULTIPLICATION: I will share what I've learned with _____.

PRAYER

Today I thank God for...

Today I am asking God for...

Review the Key Verse.

DAY 4: Psalm 63:1-8

OBSERVATION

Who?   Where?

What?   When?

How?   Why?

INTERPRETATION: What does God intend for me to learn from this passage?

APPLICATION: I will obey what is taught here by...

MULTIPLICATION: I will share what I've learned with _____.

PRAYER

Today I thank God for...

Today I am asking God for...

Review the Key Verse.

DAY 5: Psalm 46:10

OBSERVATION

Who?   Where?

What?   When?

How?   Why?

INTERPRETATION: What does God intend for me to learn from this passage?

APPLICATION: I will obey what is taught here by...

MULTIPLICATION: I will share what I've learned with _____.

PRAYER

Today I thank God for...

Today I am asking God for...

Review the Key Verse.

DAY 6: Matthew 14:22-23

OBSERVATION

Who?   Where?

What?   When?

How?   Why?

INTERPRETATION: What does God intend for me to learn from this passage?

APPLICATION: I will obey what is taught here by...

MULTIPLICATION: I will share what I've learned with _____.

PRAYER

Today I thank God for...

Today I am asking God for...

Review the Key Verse.

DAY 7: Summary and Reflection Day

After looking back over your quiet times for the week, summarize what God has been teaching you.

What specific action will you take to apply what you have learned?

PRAYER

Today I thank God for...

Today I am asking God for...

Write out this week's Key Verse below:

QUIET TIME

Answer these questions as well as you can before the Half-Time meeting. You will discuss them as a team during the Word time.

1. Why is it so important to get time alone with God on a daily basis?

2. What should take place during your quiet time?

3. What can be done to really meet with God during your quiet time and not just go through the motions?

4. Would it help you to meet with someone in the group and have your quiet times together for a period of time?

5. What is your main application from this lesson?

HALF-TIME || WEEK 7

WELCOME || 15 MINUTES

Describe the best time you ever had alone with God. Why was it so good?

WITNESS || 10 MINUTES

What did you see God do this week?

WORSHIP || 10 MINUTES

Thank God together in prayer for what he did last week.

Journal how the Lord has blessed you this week and share a few blessings with your team.

WORKS || 25 MINUTES

FISHING CHART
Update your FISHing chart with any new people you met this week or steps you took in the FISHing process.

BIG BLUE
Add your team's new friends to Big Blue. Put the list in the middle of the group and pray over your friends.

TOOLS
Pair up and practice The Bridge with another teammate, giving each other feedback.

ACTIVITY
Turn to the Game Plan on the next page and fill in your goals for this week.

WORLD || 10 MINUTES

PRAY FOR THE NATIONS

Pray for the 121 million people who live in Unreligious people groups.[2]

WORD || 20 MINUTES

Share Mark 1:35 with a partner.

Discuss your Daily Quiet Times using the Learning Questions.

Read and discuss the "Sharpening Your Skills" tip below.

SHARPENING YOUR SKILLS:
Prescriptive or Descriptive?

We are bound to follow what the Bible prescribes (the commands and principles we are all expected to do), not what the Bible describes (historical incidents that simply explain what happened). Acts 28:3-5 describes how Paul was bitten by a viper. This does not mean that we have to handle snakes. In contrast, in 1 Corinthians 11:24 we see that Jesus prescribed that we should take the Lord's Supper. This we should do in reverent obedience.

Give examples of how people break this rule.

GAME PLAN FOR NEXT WEEK

3 HOURS *with Jesus*

Daily Quiet Times and Discussion Questions
Memorize Joshua 1:8

2 HOURS *with lost people*

I will meet _____ new people this week

I will share The Bridge with _____ people this week

My ministry partner this week will be _____

1 HOUR *corporate prayer*

This week I will pray with _____

THE WORD

The Bible is God's inspired Word to man. It is infallible and completely sufficient as our guide to know him and experience life to its fullest. God's Word is food for your soul and the only trustworthy compass for direction, relationships, and ministry. Therefore, ask God to put a passion in your heart this week to study, memorize, meditate on, and obey his Word.

KEY VERSE: Joshua 1:8

DAY 1: Joshua 1:8

OBSERVATION

Who?   Where?

What?   When?

How?   Why?

INTERPRETATION: What does God intend for me to learn from this passage?

APPLICATION: I will obey what is taught here by...

MULTIPLICATION: I will share what I've learned with _____.

PRAYER

Today I thank God for...

Today I am asking God for...

Learn this week's Key Verse.

DAY 2: 2 Timothy 3:16-17

OBSERVATION

Who?   Where?

What?   When?

How?   Why?

INTERPRETATION: What does God intend for me to learn from this passage?

APPLICATION: I will obey what is taught here by...

MULTIPLICATION: I will share what I've learned with _____.

PRAYER

Today I thank God for...

Today I am asking God for...

Review the Key Verse.

DAY 3: Psalm 119:9-11

OBSERVATION

Who?   Where?

What?   When?

How?   Why?

INTERPRETATION: What does God intend for me to learn from this passage?

APPLICATION: I will obey what is taught here by...

MULTIPLICATION: I will share what I've learned with _____.

PRAYER

Today I thank God for...

Today I am asking God for...

Review the Key Verse.

DAY 4: Psalm 19:7-11

OBSERVATION

Who?   Where?

What?   When?

How?   Why?

INTERPRETATION: What does God intend for me to learn from this passage?

APPLICATION: I will obey what is taught here by...

MULTIPLICATION: I will share what I've learned with _____.

PRAYER

Today I thank God for...

Today I am asking God for...

Review the Key Verse.

DAY 5: Ezra 7:10

OBSERVATION

Who?   Where?

What?   When?

How?   Why?

INTERPRETATION: What does God intend for me to learn from this passage?

APPLICATION: I will obey what is taught here by...

MULTIPLICATION: I will share what I've learned with _____.

PRAYER

Today I thank God for...

Today I am asking God for...

Review the Key Verse.

DAY 6: Jeremiah 15:16

OBSERVATION

Who?   Where?

What?   When?

How?   Why?

INTERPRETATION: What does God intend for me to learn from this passage?

APPLICATION: I will obey what is taught here by...

MULTIPLICATION: I will share what I've learned with _____.

PRAYER

Today I thank God for...

Today I am asking God for...

Review the Key Verse.

DAY 7: Summary and Reflection Day

After looking back over your quiet times for the week, summarize what God has been teaching you.

What specific action will you take to apply what you have learned?

PRAYER

Today I thank God for...

Today I am asking God for...

Write out this week's Key Verse below:

THE WORD

Answer these questions as well as you can before the Half-Time meeting. You will discuss them as a team during the Word time.

1. What did God show you this week about his Word?

2. Do you think memorizing Scripture is important? Why or why not?

3. Do you feel like you know how to feed on God's Word? Would you like help in learning how to study the Bible better?

4. How do you plan to make the study of God's Word a priority in your life?

HALF-TIME || WEEK 8

WELCOME || 15 MINUTES

Were you more of an obedient or disobedient child growing up?

Why do you think you were the way you were?

WITNESS || 10 MINUTES

What did you see God do this week?

WORSHIP || 10 MINUTES

Thank God together in prayer for what he did last week.

Use an iPod, guitar, etc. and sing a few songs together.

WORKS || 25 MINUTES

FISHING CHART

Update your FISHing chart with any new people you met this week or steps you took in the FISHing process.

BIG BLUE

Add your team's new friends to Big Blue. Put the list in the middle of the group and pray over your friends.

TOOLS

Pair up and practice The Bridge with another teammate, giving each other feedback.

ACTIVITY

Turn to the Game Plan on the next page and fill in your goals for this week.

WORLD || 10 MINUTES

PRAY FOR THE NATIONS

Pray for the 1.3 billion people who live in Muslim people groups.[2]

WORD || 20 MINUTES

Share Joshua 1:8 with a partner.

Discuss your Daily Quiet Times using the Learning Questions.

Read and discuss the "Sharpening Your Skills" tip below.

SHARPENING YOUR SKILLS:
Principle of Surrender

Approaching God's Word with a surrendered heart is a prerequisite to understanding his will in a clear and uncorrupted way. It will help you gain a deeper level of confidence in Jesus and his teachings. Read the following passages and discuss why we must commit to do God's will before we open his Word and seek it out: Psalm 25:14, John 7:17, Eph. 4:17

GAME PLAN FOR NEXT WEEK

3 HOURS *with Jesus*

Daily Quiet Times and Discussion Questions
Memorize 1 John 5:14-15

2 HOURS *with lost people*

I will meet _____ new people this week

I will share My Story with _____ people this week

I will share The Bridge with _____ people this week

My ministry partner this week will be _____

1 HOUR *corporate prayer*

This week I will pray with _____

PRAYER

Prayer involves presenting our requests to God, but if that's all we see prayer as, we miss out on greater blessings. Communion with God himself is the most wonderful privilege available to us in prayer. Spend extra time on your knees this week pouring out your heart to God and seeking him as your greatest treasure and joy.

KEY VERSE: 1 John 5:14-15

DAY 1: 1 John 5:14-15

OBSERVATION

Who?   Where?

What?   When?

How?   Why?

INTERPRETATION: What does God intend for me to learn from this passage?

APPLICATION: I will obey what is taught here by...

MULTIPLICATION: I will share what I've learned with _____.

PRAYER

Today I thank God for...

Today I am asking God for...

Learn this week's Key Verse.

DAY 2: Philippians 4:6-7

OBSERVATION

Who?   Where?

What?   When?

How?   Why?

INTERPRETATION: What does God intend for me to learn from this passage?

APPLICATION: I will obey what is taught here by...

MULTIPLICATION: I will share what I've learned with _____.

PRAYER

Today I thank God for...

Today I am asking God for...

Review the Key Verse.

DAY 3: James 5:13-18

OBSERVATION

Who?   Where?

What?   When?

How?   Why?

INTERPRETATION: What does God intend for me to learn from this passage?

APPLICATION: I will obey what is taught here by...

MULTIPLICATION: I will share what I've learned with _____.

PRAYER

Today I thank God for...

Today I am asking God for...

Review the Key Verse.

DAY 4: Matthew 7:7-10

OBSERVATION

Who?   Where?

What?   When?

How?   Why?

INTERPRETATION: What does God intend for me to learn from this passage?

APPLICATION: I will obey what is taught here by...

MULTIPLICATION: I will share what I've learned with _____.

PRAYER

Today I thank God for...

Today I am asking God for...

Review the Key Verse.

DAY 5: Luke 18:1-8

OBSERVATION

Who?   Where?

What?   When?

How?   Why?

INTERPRETATION: What does God intend for me to learn from this passage?

APPLICATION: I will obey what is taught here by...

MULTIPLICATION: I will share what I've learned with _____.

PRAYER

Today I thank God for...

Today I am asking God for...

Review the Key Verse.

DAY 6: Matthew 21:21-22

OBSERVATION

Who?   Where?

What?   When?

How?   Why?

INTERPRETATION: What does God intend for me to learn from this passage?

APPLICATION: I will obey what is taught here by...

MULTIPLICATION: I will share what I've learned with _____.

PRAYER

Today I thank God for...

Today I am asking God for...

Review the Key Verse.

DAY 7: Summary and Reflection Day

After looking back over your quiet times for the week, summarize what God has been teaching you.

What specific action will you take to apply what you have learned?

PRAYER

Today I thank God for...

Today I am asking God for...

Write out this week's Key Verse below:

PRAYER

Answer these questions as well as you can before the Half-Time meeting. You will discuss them as a team during the Word time.

1. What did God show you this week about prayer?

2. Do you think both private and corporate prayer are important? Why or why not?

3. Do you feel like you know how to pray effectively? Would you like help in learning how to do that?

4. In what ways do you plan to make prayer a priority in your life?

HALF-TIME || WEEK 9

WELCOME || 15 MINUTES

Share about the most miraculous answer to prayer you have ever seen.

WITNESS || 10 MINUTES

What did you see God do this week?

WORSHIP || 10 MINUTES

Thank God together in prayer for what he did last week.

Take turns reading a few verses of Psalm 145, stopping to praise God for who he is and what he does.

WORKS || 25 MINUTES

FISHING CHART
Update your FISHing chart with any new people you met this week or steps you took in the FISHing process.

BIG BLUE
Add your team's new friends to Big Blue. Put the list in the middle of the group and pray over your friends.

TOOLS
Pair up and practice The Bridge with another teammate, giving each other feedback.

ACTIVITY
Turn to the Game Plan on the next page and fill in your goals for this week.

WORLD || 10 MINUTES

PRAY FOR THE NATIONS
Pray for the 275 million people who live in Buddhist people groups.[2]

WORD || 20 MINUTES

Share 1 John 5:14-15 with a partner.

Discuss your Daily Quiet Times using the Learning Questions.

Read and discuss the "Sharpening Your Skills" tip below.

SHARPENING YOUR SKILLS:
Arguments from Silence

Some churches believe it is unscriptural to use musical instruments in worship. Their reasoning is that since the book of Acts does not mention the use of musical instruments, it must be wrong to use them. Discuss why it is dangerous territory to base your beliefs and practices off of what the Bible doesn't say, rather than what it does say.

GAME PLAN FOR NEXT WEEK

3 HOURS *with Jesus*

Daily Quiet Times and Discussion Questions
Memorize Zechariah 4:6

2 HOURS *with lost people*

This week, the evangelistic activity I will do is _____
(meet new people, share The Bridge, share My Story)

I will do an evangelistic activity with _____ people this week

My ministry partner this week will be _____

1 HOUR *corporate prayer*

This week I will pray with _____

LIFE IN THE SPIRIT

Jesus has not left us alone. He sends his Spirit to live inside his children. His Spirit empowers us to live supernaturally. The Spirit teaches and reminds us of truth that sets us free from sin and enables us to experience love, joy, peace, etc. in our daily lives. When we ignore his promptings, we quench his influence in our lives, and he is grieved. Confession and repentance (deciding to turn away from sin) can restore our fellowship with the Spirit and bring times of refreshing and renewed power. Failing to learn how to walk in the power of the Holy Spirit stunts our spiritual growth and reduces our impact on the world. Set your heart this week on learning how to appropriate the Spirit's power in your life.

KEY VERSE TO MEMORIZE: Zechariah 4:6

DAY 1: Galatians 5:22-26

OBSERVATION

Who?   Where?

What?   When?

How?   Why?

INTERPRETATION: What does God intend for me to learn from this passage?

APPLICATION: I will obey what is taught here by...

MULTIPLICATION: I will share what I've learned with _____.

PRAYER

Today I thank God for...

Today I am asking God for...

Learn this week's Key Verse.

DAY 2: Ephesians 4:30, 1 Thessalonians 5:19

OBSERVATION

Who?   Where?

What?   When?

How?   Why?

INTERPRETATION: What does God intend for me to learn from this passage?

APPLICATION: I will obey what is taught here by...

MULTIPLICATION: I will share what I've learned with _____.

PRAYER

Today I thank God for...

Today I am asking God for...

Review the Key Verse.

DAY 3: Ephesians 5:18-21

OBSERVATION

    Who?   Where?

    What?   When?

    How?   Why?

INTERPRETATION: What does God intend for me to learn from this passage?

APPLICATION: I will obey what is taught here by...

MULTIPLICATION: I will share what I've learned with _____.

PRAYER

Today I thank God for...

Today I am asking God for...

Review the Key Verse.

DAY 4: John 8:32, 14:25-26, 16:12-16

OBSERVATION

    Who?   Where?

    What?   When?

    How?   Why?

INTERPRETATION: What does God intend for me to learn from this passage?

APPLICATION: I will obey what is taught here by...

MULTIPLICATION: I will share what I've learned with _____.

PRAYER

Today I thank God for...

Today I am asking God for...

Review the Key Verse.

DAY 5: Mark 13:10-11, Acts 1:8

OBSERVATION

Who?   Where?

What?   When?

How?   Why?

INTERPRETATION: What does God intend for me to learn from this passage?

APPLICATION: I will obey what is taught here by...

MULTIPLICATION: I will share what I've learned with _____.

PRAYER

Today I thank God for...

Today I am asking God for...

Review the Key Verse.

DAY 6: Zechariah 4:6

OBSERVATION

Who?   Where?

What?   When?

How?   Why?

INTERPRETATION: What does God intend for me to learn from this passage?

APPLICATION: I will obey what is taught here by...

MULTIPLICATION: I will share what I've learned with _____.

PRAYER

Today I thank God for...

Today I am asking God for...

Review the Key Verse.

DAY 7: Summary and Reflection Day

After looking back over your quiet times for the week, summarize what God has been teaching you.

What specific action will you take to apply what you have learned?

PRAYER

Today I thank God for...

Today I am asking God for...

Write this week's Key Verse below:

LIFE IN THE SPIRIT

Answer these questions as well as you can before the Half-Time meeting. You will discuss them as a team during the Word time.

1. What does the Holy Spirit do that helps us experience freedom?

2. How does one walk and keep in step with the Spirit?

3. What does it mean to grieve or quench the Holy Spirit? What should you do when you realize that you have grieved or quenched the Spirit?

4. Fresh fillings of the Spirit of God in your life come from fresh surrenders. Is there an area of your life that you need to surrender afresh to the Lordship of Christ?

5. Who would benefit from you sharing what you learned this week?

HALF-TIME || WEEK 10

WELCOME || 15 MINUTES

Who is the person you know who most displays the Spirit of Jesus? Describe briefly what they are like.

WITNESS || 10 MINUTES

What did you see God do this week?

WORSHIP || 10 MINUTES

Thank God together in prayer for what he did last week.

Take turns reading a few verses of Psalm 98, stopping to praise God for who he is and what he does.

WORKS || 25 MINUTES

FISHING CHART
Update your FISHing chart with any new people you met this week or steps you took in the FISHing process.

BIG BLUE
Add your team's new friends to Big Blue. Spend an extended time praying for all of your friends on this list.

TOOLS
Pair up and practice The Bridge with another teammate, giving each other feedback.

ACTIVITY
Turn to the Game Plan on the next page and fill in your goals for this week.

WORLD || 10 MINUTES

PRAY FOR THE NATIONS
Pray for the 1.2 billion people who live in India.[1]

WORD || 20 MINUTES

Share Zechariah 4:6 with a partner.

Discuss your Daily Quiet Times using the Learning Questions.

Read and discuss the "Sharpening Your Skills" tip below.

SHARPENING YOUR SKILLS:
Principle of Objective Interpretation

Interpret your experience in light of Scripture, not Scripture in light of your experience. For example, because the Bible is inspired by God, it would be wrong to say, "I have never seen a miracle, so miracles like those in the Bible must have ceased." Instead, one should study the Bible and see what God says about the continuation of miracles. What examples can you think of where people mistakenly interpret the Bible in light of their experiences?

GAME PLAN FOR NEXT WEEK

3 HOURS *with Jesus*

Daily Quiet Times and Discussion Questions
Memorize Hebrews 12:2

2 HOURS *with lost people*

This week, the evangelistic activity I will do is _____
(meet new people, share The Bridge, share My Story)

I will do an evangelistic activity with _____ people this week

My ministry partner this week will be _____

1 HOUR *corporate prayer*

This week I will pray with _____

PERSEVERANCE IN SUFFERING

Suffering is a fact of life. Both Christians and non-Christians experience pain. The question is not, will you have hardship in life, but how well will you suffer. Will you allow God to fill you with joy, even though you experience difficulties? Will you bring him glory in your suffering and grow as a result of it? Or will you gripe, give up, and become bitter? The choice is yours.

His power will enable you to endure well if you will turn to him in your time of need. The Bible has a lot to say about suffering. Determine to learn all you can this week to prepare yourself to persevere and glorify God in your sufferings.

KEY VERSE: Hebrews 12:2

DAY 1: Hebrews 12:1-13

OBSERVATION

Who?   Where?

What?   When?

How?   Why?

INTERPRETATION: What does God intend for me to learn from this passage?

APPLICATION: I will obey what is taught here by...

MULTIPLICATION: I will share what I've learned with _____.

PRAYER

Today I thank God for...

Today I am asking God for...

Learn this week's Key Verse.

DAY 2: 1 Corinthians 15:54-58

OBSERVATION

Who?   Where?

What?   When?

How?   Why?

INTERPRETATION: What does God intend for me to learn from this passage?

APPLICATION: I will obey what is taught here by...

MULTIPLICATION: I will share what I've learned with _____.

PRAYER

Today I thank God for...

Today I am asking God for...

Review the Key Verse.

DAY 3: John 15:18-21, Matthew 10:16-23

OBSERVATION

Who?   Where?

What?   When?

How?   Why?

INTERPRETATION: What does God intend for me to learn from this passage?

APPLICATION: I will obey what is taught here by...

MULTIPLICATION: I will share what I've learned with _____.

PRAYER

Today I thank God for...

Today I am asking God for...

Review the Key Verse.

DAY 4: 2 Corinthians 4:16-18, James 1:2-4

OBSERVATION

Who?   Where?

What?   When?

How?   Why?

INTERPRETATION: What does God intend for me to learn from this passage?

APPLICATION: I will obey what is taught here by...

MULTIPLICATION: I will share what I've learned with _____.

PRAYER

Today I thank God for...

Today I am asking God for...

Review the Key Verse.

DAY 5: 1 Peter 4:12-13

OBSERVATION

Who?   Where?

What?   When?

How?   Why?

INTERPRETATION: What does God intend for me to learn from this passage?

APPLICATION: I will obey what is taught here by...

MULTIPLICATION: I will share what I've learned with _____.

PRAYER

Today I thank God for...

Today I am asking God for...

Review the Key Verse.

DAY 6: Hebrews 10:32-39, Hebrews 11:24-27

OBSERVATION

Who?   Where?

What?   When?

How?   Why?

INTERPRETATION: What does God intend for me to learn from this passage?

APPLICATION: I will obey what is taught here by...

MULTIPLICATION: I will share what I've learned with _____.

PRAYER

Today I thank God for...

Today I am asking God for...

Review the Key Verse.

DAY 7: Summary and Reflection Day

After looking back over your quiet times for the week, summarize what God has been teaching you.

What specific action will you take to apply what you have learned?

PRAYER

Today I thank God for...

Today I am asking God for...

Write out this week's Key Verse below:

PERSEVERANCE IN SUFFERING

Answer these questions as well as you can before the Half-Time meeting. You will discuss them as a team during the Word time.

1. Why do you think the scriptures put so much emphasis on building the expectation that we will experience suffering?

2. What were some key things you noticed in the verses you studied this week that will help you persevere in tough times?

3. What attitudes are important to maintain while you are going through a period of suffering?

4. How will you apply what you learned this week?

WELCOME || 15 MINUTES

If you have thirty minutes of free time, how do you spend it?

WITNESS || 10 MINUTES

What did you see God do this week?

WORSHIP || 10 MINUTES

Thank God together in prayer for what he did last week.

Use an iPod, guitar, etc. and sing a few songs together.

WORKS || 25 MINUTES

FISHING CHART
Update your FISHing chart with any new people you met this week or steps you took in the FISHing process.

BIG BLUE
Add your team's new friends to Big Blue. Put the list in the middle of the group and pray over your friends.

TOOLS
Pair up and practice The Bridge with another teammate, giving each other feedback.

WORLD || 10 MINUTES

PRAY FOR THE NATIONS
Pray for the 1.3 billion people who live in China.[2]

WORD || 20 MINUTES

Share Hebrews 12:2 with a partner.

Discuss your Daily Quiet Times using the Learning Questions.

Read and discuss the "Sharpening Your Skills" tip below.

> **SHARPENING YOUR SKILLS:**
> Principle of Community
>
> While every believer has the right and responsibility to study God's Word for himself, there can be great protection in interacting with other believers in the process. Read 1 Corinthians 14:29-31 and discuss the benefits of corporate Bible study.

APPENDIX

FISHing Chart
My Story: Interest-Creating Testimony
FIND: Questions
The Legend of Big Blue
Matthew Party
Bridge Illustration
Sharing the Vision for Multiplication

FISHING CHART

#	Name	FIND						INTEREST				SHARE				HELP	
		Interests	Felt Needs	Attitude Toward Jesus	Testimony	Answered Prayer Stories	Exposure to Christian Community	Prayer for their needs	Discovery Bible Study	Gospel Presentation	Give Them Something to Read	Ask for a Decision	Deal with Barriers
1													
2													
3													
4													
5													
6													
7													
8													
9													
10													

FISHING CHART

#	Name	FIND				INTEREST					SHARE			HELP	
		Interests	Felt Needs	Attitude Toward Jesus	Testimony	Answered Prayer Stories	Exposure to Christian Community	Prayer for their needs	Discovery Bible Study	Gospel Presentation	Give Them Something to Read	Ask for a Decision	Deal with Barriers
1													
2													
3													
4													
5													
6													
7													
8													
9													
10													

MY STORY: INTEREST-CREATING TESTIMONY

I first sensed my need for Jesus when…

What made me most interested in Jesus was…

I finally decided to trust Jesus and follow him when I realized that…

Since I entered into a relationship with Jesus, I have changed

From: To:

From: To:

Jesus helps me in my daily life by…

I have seen God answer my prayers in some pretty cool ways like the time…

_____, have you ever considered learning about how to follow Jesus?

FIND: QUESTIONS

When meeting a new person, the easiest way to begin getting to know him or her is by asking questions. It is usually best to start by asking biographical questions before asking more personal questions concerning their interests and needs. Take a minute to read over the following example questions. Then take turns practicing asking questions and moving the conversation from biographical to interests to needs.

1. **Biographical questions**

    Where are you from?

    Where do you live now?

    What do you do?

    Tell me about your family.

2. **Interests questions** (Hopefully, these questions will help you find some ways you can spend time with them in the future.)

    Do you have any hobbies or favorite sports?

    What is your favorite thing to do in your free time?

3. **Needs questions**

    I try to pray for the needs of people I meet. Is there anything specific I can pray for you?

THE LEGEND OF BIG BLUE

In 2007, a dedicated group of believers in Iowa began to meet as a missional community. A cornerstone of their weekly meetings was a time of prayer for the lost. Names of lost friends were written on a leftover piece of blue flooring material, which was then laid in the middle of the room to be prayed over. Each week, as members recalled people they had met, new names were added to the list. A time of intense prayer would follow as disciples got on their knees to pray over "Big Blue." As these groups multiplied and spread to other states, so did the inclusion of Big Blue. Get a blue piece of fabric or poster board and join the movement!

MATTHEW PARTY

A Matthew Party is a get-together planned for people who need to meet Jesus. We get the name from Matthew, the tax collector, who held a reception in his home for people to come meet Jesus. One of the goals of this event is to allow our lost friends to experience the difference Christ makes in a community of believers. It is important that we aren't outnumbered, as seeing Christ-centered community in action is the goal behind this gathering. We want them to see the love we have for one another. A Matthew Party can be a dinner, a game night, bowling, ice skating, some sort of cultural activity, etc. The important thing is allowing our lost friends to spend time with a group of believers.

LUKE 5:29-32 (ESV)

And Levi [Matthew] made him [Jesus] a great feast in his house, and there was a large company of tax collectors and others reclining at table with them. And the Pharisees and their scribes grumbled at his disciples, saying, "Why do you eat and drink with tax collectors and sinners?"

And Jesus answered them, "Those who are well have no need of a physician, but those who are sick. I have not come to call the righteous but sinners to repentance."

JOHN 13:35

By this all people will know that you are my disciples, if you have love for one another.

THE BRIDGE ILLUSTRATION

If you need a video demonstration of The Bridge, several good versions can be found online.

THE BRIDGE ILLUSTRATION

SHARING THE VISION FOR MULTIPLICATION *(FILLED IN)*

YOUR POTENTIAL IMPACT

If you only discipled two people per year and taught them to teach others to multiply each year, you could multiply over 3 Billion disciples in just twenty years.

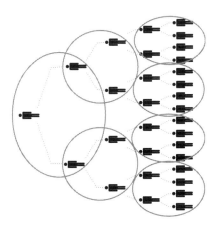

☐ Draw circles around groups of disciples and discuss the importance of multiplying not only disciples, but disciple-making teams.

WHAT ACTION WILL YOU TAKE?

☐ I will seek out someone to disciple me.

☐ I will seek out people to disciple.

WHAT PAUL DID

"And what you have heard from me in the presence of many witnesses entrust to faithful men who will be able to teach others also."

2 Timothy 2:2

Paul — Titus
Silas
Timothy — faithful
faithful
faithful men — faithful
others
others
others

WHAT JESUS DID

Jesus

The Twelve

Inner _Circle_

Peter
James
John

WHAT JESUS COMMANDED

"Therefore go and _make_ _disciples_ of _all_ _nations_, baptizing them in the name of the Father and of the Son and of the Holy Spirit."

Matthew 28:19

WHAT JESUS PROMISED

"Others, like seed sown on good soil, hear the word, accept it, and produce a crop—some _30_, some _60_, some _100_ times what was sown."

Mark 4:20

SHARING THE VISION FOR MULTIPLICATION

WHAT JESUS DID

The Twelve

Peter
James
John

Inner _____

WHAT JESUS COMMANDED

"Therefore go and _____ of _____, baptizing them in the name of the Father and of the Son and of the Holy Spirit."

Matthew 28:19

WHAT JESUS PROMISED

"Others, like seed sown on good soil, hear the word, accept it, and produce a crop— some _____, some _____, some _____ times what was sown."

Mark 4:20

WHAT PAUL DID

"And what you have heard from me in the presence of many witnesses entrust to faithful men who will be able to teach others also."

2 Timothy 2:2

Paul

Silas

Titus

YOUR POTENTIAL IMPACT

If you only discipled two people per year and taught them to teach others to multiply each year, you could multiply over 3 _____ disciples in just twenty years.

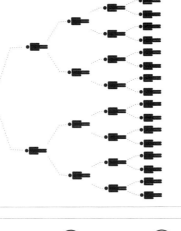

☐ Draw circles around groups of disciples and discuss the importance of multiplying not only disciples, but disciple-making teams.

WHAT ACTION WILL YOU TAKE?

☐ I will seek out someone to disciple me.

☐ I will seek out people to disciple.

SPIRITUAL MULTIPLICATION IN THE REAL WORLD

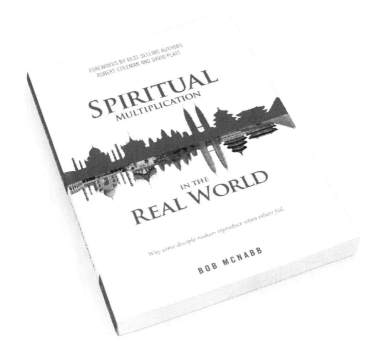

This ministry resource is designed to equip believers with an arsenal of biblical principles for a fruitful ministry of evangelism and disciple-making, no matter the context in which they reside. When read along with its companion study guide, *Spiritual Multiplication in the Real World* gives small groups direction on how to immediately apply what they are learning. They don't just read about disciple-making teams; they become one! Groups who read the book and use its study guide can expect to gain the following:

- Vision for spiritual multiplication and how God can impact the world through you
- Commitment to biblical community and teamwork
- Excitement for evangelism that everyone can do
- An overview of the disciple-making process and practical knowledge of how to move disciples from new birth to maturity to reproduction

BULK PRICING AVAILABLE AT SPIRITUALMULTIPLICATION.ORG

MISSIONAL COMMUNITY STUDY GUIDE

AN EQUIPPING TOOL

Merely reading about how your group can be a disciple-making team is very different from actually becoming one. Designed for established disciples seeking to be equipped, this *Missional Community Study Guide* is a companion to *Spiritual Multiplication in the Real World* and will help you and your group function as a reproducing *team*. It will direct you week by week into high impact habits, both individually and corporately, propelling you beyond simply making disciples to making disciple-*makers*. This guidebook has proven to be ideal for helping believers who are established in their walks with Christ to become equipped to labor as multipliers in his kingdom.

BULK PRICING AVAILABLE AT SPIRITUALMULTIPLICATION.ORG

ENDNOTES

1 Joshua Project, *www.joshuaproject.org*

2 *The Task Remaining* by Ralph D. Winter and Bruce A. Koch, *Perspectives on the World Christian Movement, Reader.* 4th ed. William Carey Library, 2009, p.531-546. *www.missionbooks.org*

3 *The Coming Revolution: Because Status Quo Missions Won't Finish the Job* by Mark R. Baxter, Tate Publishing, 2007, p.12.

4 The Traveling Team, *www.thetravelingteam.org*

5 Statistics from The Institute of International Education, Inc. *www.iie.org*

6 Statistics from *www.wycliffe.org/about/statistics.aspx*

Made in the USA
Columbia, SC
07 March 2021